Dad
Jokes

What happens when you put
your hand in a blender?

You get a hand shake.

My wife complains I don't buy
her flowers.

To be honest, I didn't know
she sold flowers.

What color is the wind?

Blew.

What do you call a typo on a tombstone?

A grave mistake.

There can be 100 people in a room and 99 won't slap you.

But one Will.

I was having trouble with my Internet at the farm, so I moved the modem to the barn.

Now I have stable wifi.

What do you call a cow in
an earthquake?

A milkshake.

Every single morning I get hit by
the same bike...

It's a vicious cycle...

Just so everybody's clear.

I'm going to put my glasses on.

What do clouds wear?

Thunder wear.

Three conspiracy theorists
walk into a bar.

You can't tell me that's
a coincidence!

What do you call a zombie who
writes music?

A decomposer.

I'm a social vegan...

I'm avoiding meets.

Interviewer: Describe yourself
in 3 words.

"Not good at counting".

I once had a job with the zoo,
circumsizing elephants.

It didn't pay very much, but
the tips were huge.

What did the drummer call his twin daughters?

Anna One, Anna Two.

What's the difference between a ruble and a dollar?

A dollar.

Never share a secret with a clock.

Time will tell.

I applied for a job hanging mirrors.

It's something I can see myself doing.

I just figured out why Teslas are so expensive.

It's because they charge a lot.

What did the carpenter say when he finished building his house?

Nailed it.

I'm not saying I'm attractive, but when I take my clothes off in the bathroom.

I turn the shower on.

How did the hacker get away from the police?

He ransomware.

My wife apologised for the first time ever today.

She said she's sorry she ever married me.

My wife claims that a man in camouflage is really sexy.

I just don't see it.

What do you call detective who just solves cases accidentally?

Sheer Luck Holmes.

How does a hamburger introduce his girlfriend?

Meet Patty.

97% of people are stupid.

Thank God I'm in the other 5%.

In Britain they call it a "lift" but Americans call it an "elevator".

I guess we're just raised differently.

You think gas prices are expensive, have you seen Chimneys?

They're through the roof.

A vampires favorite ship.

Is a blood vessel.

6:30 is the best time on
the clock,

Hands down.

The man who invented Velcro
has died.

RIP.

Not sure if my sister knows any geography.

But Alaska.

Can everyone who is here for the yodelling lessons...

Please form an orderly orderly orderly orderly queue.

My friends love scaring the crap out of me.

With friends like that who needs enemas?

I'm in a band called Dyslexia.

We've just released our
Greatest Shit album.

I asked my German friend if he
knew the square root of 81.

He said no.

My last wife said I was
unnecessarily mysterious.

Or did she?

My cloning experiment is finally a success.

I'm so excited; I'm beside myself!

I once had a hen that could count her own eggs.

She was a mathemachicken.

People call me self centred.

But that's enough about them.

I had to fire my fruit delivery driver today.

I hate to let the mango but he was driving me bananas.

My favourite teacher back in school was Mrs Turtle.

Funny name, but she tortoise well.

I wrote a book on how to fall down the stairs.

It's a step by step guide.

I have the attention of a goldfish.

Seriously, it's been watching
me for hours.

Why is it a bad idea to iron your
four-leaf clover?

Because you shouldn't
press your luck.

I met a beautiful woman in the
museum in Paris.

I think I'm in Louvre.

There are 4 quarters in
the Superbowl.

And that's why they brought
out 50 Cent at halftime.

Did you know milk is the
fastest liquid in the universe?

Before you see it, it's
already pasteurized.

What do you call a woman who
can't make sandwiches?

Single.

Did you hear about the pole vault champion of North Korea?

He's now the pole vault champion of South Korea.

To everyone out there suffering from paranoia.

Just remember you're not alone.

What do you call a man in debt?

Owen.

What do computers eat?

Micro chips!

What did the shipmates find
in the toilet?

The Captain's Log.

My friend decided to become
an archeologist

...now his life is in ruins.

I told my girlfriend I think she's cheating on me.

She told me I sound just like her husband.

Two mice chewing on a film roll.

One of them goes: "I think the book was better."

Went to the doctor's today, he told me I was going deaf.

That news was hard for me to hear.

My wife is blaming me for ruining her birthday.

That's ridiculous, I didn't even know it was her birthday.

My friend Tony asked me not to say his name backwards.

I said y not?

Someone tried to sell me a coffin today.

I said that's the last thing I need.

T-shirt is actually short for tyrannosaurus shirt.

It's because of the small arms.

My wife asked me:
"What starts with F and ends in K."

I said: "No it doesn't."

I asked my wife if I was the only one she'd been with.

She said yes, all the others had been nines and tens.

Someone asked me to name
two structures that hold water.

I was like well damn.

Yesterday a clown held a
door open for me.

I thought it was a nice jester.

Can someone please tell me
what LGBTQ+ stands for?

Nobody is giving me a straight answer.

Somebody said my dad's gay.

And now I'm trying to work out which one.

I'm not fan of elevator music.

It is bad on so many levels.

How does music say goodbye?

Audios!

I've trained my dog to go
and fetch me a bottle of wine.

He's a Bordeaux collie.

We started a band and
called it "Books".

So no one can judge us
by our covers.

I ran into my friend Mark who
stole my dictionary.

I said, "Mark, my words!"

Never shout into a colander.

It'll strain your voice.

I asked the professor "What happened before The Big Bang?"

He said, "Sorry. No Time."

My grandfather was always terrible until I had my first child.

Now he's a great grandfather.

My wife asked me to put ketchup on the shopping list.

Now I can't read anything.

Waiter: How do you like your steak, sir?

Sir: Like winning an argument with my wife.

Waiter: Rare it is.

What's brown and sticky?

A stick.

How much does a Grandpa
weigh?

Usually a little more than
a Gram.

Can anyone tell me what
oblivious means?

I have no idea.

What do you call a zombie who
doesn't joke around?

Dead serious.

What happens when you hit Dwayne Johnsons butt?

You hit Rock bottom.

I kept wondering why the ball was getting bigger.

And then it hit me.

A bossy man goes into a bar.

He orders everyone a round.

I have a friend who really hates living in Central USA.

She says she's in a constant state of Missouri.

Did you hear about the restaurant called Karma?

There's no menu. You get what you deserve.

Did you hear about the Giant with diarrhea?

It's all over town.

I am so poor.

I can't even pay attention.

I know loads of jokes about
cash machines.

I just can't think of one atm.

I had a date last night, it
was perfect.

Tomorrow I'll try a grape.

Stephen King has a son
named Joe.

I'm not JO-king, but he is.

I turned down a job where I
would be paid in vegetables.

The celery was unacceptable.

Why should we never trust stairs?

Because they are always
up to something.

I haven't spoken to my wife
in 7 years.

I don't want to interrupt her.

Me: I'm not saying a word without
my lawyer present.

Cop: You ARE the lawyer.

Lawyer: So where's my present?

I always keep my guitar in
the car now.

It's good for traffic jams.

"Dad, can I eat the cake in the fridge?"

"Sure, but the dining room would probably be more comfortable."

My twin brother called me from prison.

He said: "You know how we finish each other's sentences?"

Scientists have just discovered a fossilised dinosaur fart.

They say it's a blast from the past.

I asked my friend Sam to sing a song about the iPhone.

And then Samsung.

I told my wife she was drawing her eyebrows too high.

She looked surprised.

I got mugged by six dwarves last night.

Not happy.

If the Pope were to bless an avocado...

...would that make it holy guacamole?

How do you console an English teacher?

There, their, they're

I told my wife she needs to start embracing her mistakes.

So she hugged me.

What do you call a woman who's really good at darts?

Amy.

What's blue and smells like red paint?

Blue paint.

Why did the Mexican take anti-anxiety medication?

For hispanic attacks.

I didn't last very long in my last job as a human cannonball...

I was fired.

What dating app do lumberjacks use?

Timber.

I have a fear of overly intricate buildings...

I have a complex complex complex.

I've got this disease where I can't stop making airport puns.

The doctor says it terminal.

What's an astronaut's favorite part of the computer?

The Space Bar.

How do you jump higher on a water bed?

You fill it with spring water.

Why can't blind people eat fish?

It's sea food.

What's the most effective way to remember your wife's birthday?

Forget it once.

A pun walks into a room and kills ten people.

Pun in, ten dead.

What did the bra say to
the hat?

You go on a head, I'll give
these two a lift.

If a Viking is reincarnated,

Is he Bjorn again?

What did Spartacus say when
the lion ate his wife?

Nothing, he was gladiator.

After all these years, my wife
still thinks I'm sexy.

Every time I walk by she
says: "What an ass!"

The first rule of passive
aggressive club is...

You know what, nevermind.
It's fine.

What do you call a fat psychic?

A 4 chin teller.

I'm developing a new fragrance for introverts.

It's called: "Leave me the fuh cologne."

My wife asked me "is it just me or is the cat getting fat?"

Apparently "no it's just you" wasn't the right answer.

What's the difference between a simple person and a pizza?

One is easy to cheat, the other is cheesy to eat.

Just got hospitalised due to a peekaboo accident.

They put me in the ICU.

What did Jay-Z call his wife before they got married?

Feyonce.

What do you call a Magician who lost his magic?

ian.

How do cows stay
up to date?

They read the Moo-spaper.

When the doctor told
me that there
was a cure for dyslexia,

It was music to my arse!

What did Adam say to the
missus on the 24th of December?

It's Christmas Eve.

How much does Santa
pay to park his sleigh?

Nothing, it's on the house.

Is "buttcheeks" one word?

Or should I spread them apart?

What did the cannibal
choose as his last meal?

Five guys.

I shortened the rope on the bucket used to collect the village's water.

Didn't go down well.

I have bought my wife a fridge for Christmas.

I can't wait to see her face light up when she opens it.

What fish is made out of two sodium atoms?

2 Na.

**How does a train hear
another train coming?**

With its engineers.

Never ever spell part backwards.

It's a trap.

I just crashed my new Kia.

Now I have Nokia.

My books fell out of the bookcase.

I only have my shelf
to blame.

What do a tick and Eiffel Tower
have in common?

They are both Paris sites.

I'm opening a chain of Elvis
themed steak restaurants...

It will be for people who
love meat tender.

My wife just called
me pretentious.

I was so surprised my
monocle fell out.

How can anyone think the
Academy Awards are real?

I watched it and it's obvious that
everyone there is a paid actor!

You know what they say about
cold spaghetti.

Those who forget the pasta
are doomed to reheat it.

My wife says I'm cheap...

... But I'm not buying it.

Why don't pirates take a shower
before they walk the plank?

They just wash up on shore.

I only recently found out that
Albert Einstein was a real person..

All this time I thought he was
only a theoretical physicist.

Why do the Norwegians put barcodes on their battleships?

So they can Scandinavian.

Bruce Lee was fast.

His brother Sudden Lee was faster.

Why do jocks play on artificial turf?

To keep them from grazing.

My wife thinks I don't give her enough privacy.

At least that's what she said in her diary.

How do you make the number one disappear?

You just add a G and it's gone.

My friend has designed an invisible aeroplane.

I can't see it taking off.

Poop jokes aren't my favorite.

But they're a solid
number two.

I spent $80 on a belt that
didn't fit.

My wife said it was a
huge waist.

Just learned the word for
constipation in German.

Farfrompoopen.

I told my wife she should
embrace her mistakes.

She gave me a hug.

My new sweater had a problem
with static so I returned it.

They gave me a new one
free of charge.

How would a proud computer
dad introduce his son?

A microchip off the old block.

Thinking of having my ashes stored in a glass urn.

Remains to be seen.

They warned me not to lean over the edge of that tower in Paris.

Eiffel.

What's the least spoken language in the world?

Sign language.

What happens when you
eat aluminium foil?

You sheet metal.

I recently joined a nudist colony.

**The first week was
the hardest.**

My Viagra addiction...

**Was the hardest time
of my life.**

So what if I don't know what apocalypse means?

Its not the end of the world.

I just burnt my Hawaiian Pizza.

Should have used aloha temperature.

Vin Diesel eats two meals a day.

Breakfast and breakfurious.

What do you call a beehive
without an exit?

Unbeeleaveable!

Some people have trouble
sleeping.

But I can do it with my
eyes closed.

What do you call a sad cup
of coffee?

Depresso.

What kind of a bee can't make up its mind?

A maybee!

What is the opposite of a croissant.

A Happy Uncle.

I accidentally rubbed ketchup in my eyes.

I now have Heinzsight.

Why can't drummers come
back from retirement?

Because there will
be repercussions.

I met a girl with 12 breasts.
Seems strange.

Dozen tit?

A priest, an atheist, and a
rabbit walk into a bar.

And the rabbit says, "Guys, I'm
pretty sure I'm a typo."

Why couldn't anyone understand
the retired perfume maker?

Because he no longer
made scents.

I've started saying mucho
to my Mexican friends.

It means a lot to them.

I tried to climb a really tall
tower in France...

...but Eiffel off.

What do you call a letter from a feminist?

Hate male.

Saw a squirrel that couldn't make up his mind today.

He was on the fence all day.

I want to tell you about a woman who eats plants

You've probably never heard of herbivore...

What do you call a man
with half a brain?

Gifted.

When's the only time you
can change a man?

When he's a baby.

What's the difference between a pit
bull and a woman with PMS?

Lipstick.

A B-flat, a E-flat and a G-flat
walk into a bar.

The bartender says "Sorry
I don't serve minors".

Where do couples go in the
mall to argue?

The fued court.

What do you get when you drop
a piano down a mine shaft?

A flat minor.

Dogs can't operate MRI machines

But Catscan

What do you call nitrogen that
just finished eating?

Nitrate.

What's the best way to watch
a fly fishing tournament?

Live stream.

What do lawyers wear to work?

Law suits...

How do two arsonists hook up?

A match on tinder.

How are rotten eggs like dads?

They both have bad yolks.

Stop kink shaming America for
not using metric.

We have a foot fetish.
Grow up.

When I die I want my ashes placed
into an hourglass for my family.

So they can check on
me time after time.

What kind of Dr. is Dr. Pepper?

He's a Fizzician.

How can you tell a man is thinking about sex?

He's breathing.

How do you say "No TV" in Russia?

Nietflix.

If the number 666 is considered evil

25.8069758 is the root of all evil.

What do you call a man who marries another man?

A priest.

Not all math jokes are terrible

only sum

Why do archaeologists get all the girls?

Because they have the best dating techniques.

How do you tell when a
man is lying?

His lips move.

How do you tell an old man?

It's not hard.

How many men does it take to
replace the toilet roll?

Don't know, it's
never happened.

How do you bring a sparkle
to a man's eyes?

Shine a torch in
his ear.

Why are men like
commercials?

You can't believe a
word they say.

Why are men like blenders?

You need one, but you're
not quite sure why.

I made a graph showing all
my past relationships.

It has an ex-axis and
a why-axis.

I accidentally drank a bottle of
invisible ink last night.

I'm in the hospital now,
waiting to be seen.

Why do bees stay in their beehives
all through the winter?

Swarm.

Someone threw a bottle of mayonnaise at me.

I said, "What the hellmann?"

What do you call a caveman who is walking really slowly?

A Meanderthal.

Did you hear about the Pharaoh who was arrested?

He was involved in a pyramid scheme.

I accidently sprayed deodorant in my mouth.

Now when I talk I have this weird axe scent.

What did the hat say to the scarf?

You hang around. I'll go on ahead.

So many people are too judgemental these days.

I can tell just by looking at them.

A storm blew away 25% of my
roof last night.

oof.

Lance isn't a common name
these days.

But in medieval times, people
were named Lance a lot.

If you're unable to hold your
bladder in the Netherlands...

...European.

I've just invented the first thought controlled air freshener...

It makes scents when you think about it.

Which US state has the highest laundry detergent usage?

Washington.

When my wife is depressed I let her color in my tattoos.

She just wanted a shoulder to crayon.

What brand of underwear
do scientists wear?

Kelvin Klein.

The only thing that flat-earthers
have to fear...

Is sphere itself.

What's green and not heavy?

Light green.

What do you call a
handcuffed man?

Trustworthy.

What's the difference between
government bonds and men?

Bonds mature.

What's the difference between
a man and E.T.?

E.T. phoned home.

What do you call a man with 99% of his brain missing?

Castrated.

How many men does it take to wallpaper a room?

It depends how thinly you slice them.

How do you turn a fox into an elephant?

Marry her.

How does the Man in the Moon
cut his hair?

Eclipse it!

The Earth is 70% uncarbonated
water

Therefore the Earth is flat.

When you die what part of
the body dies last?

The pupils because they dilate.

Why do clumsy farmers make good DJs?

They're always dropping the beets.

How did the tree access the internet?

It "logged" on.

What do you call a snake without any clothing?

S-naked.

How does a nonbinary
samurai kill people?

They slash them.

A friend of mine kept annoying
me with puns about birds.

But I taught him Toucan
play that game!

Just spent $100 on a belt
that doesn't fit!

Huge waist.

What do you call a women with
one leg longer than the other?

Eileen.

Did you hear what happened
to the wooden car?

It wooden go.

I asked my wife why we
never talk about gravity.

She said it just never
seems to come up.

What car would Jesus drive if
he were alive today?

A Christler.

What did the right eye say
to the left eye?

Between you and me,
something smells.

What do you call James Bond
taking a bath?

Bubble 07.

I fell in my driveway and
can't sue anyone.

It was my own asphalt.

Did you know that plateaus...

Are the highest form
of flattery?

What's the worst thing to say
before a driving exam?

"This thing does have
airbags, right?"

How do gamers like to shower?

With Steam.

Why do the numbers 3 and
5 make such a great team?

Because together
they thrive.

I only know one bad pun
about paper.

It's tearable.

What has five toes
and isn't your foot?

My foot.

What has 4 wheels and flies?

A garbage truck.

Why do seagulls fly over the sea?

Because if they flew over
the bay, they'd be bagels!

I hate it when my wife gets
mad at me for being lazy.

It's not like I did anything!

What's the difference between
a hippo and a zippo?

One is really heavy and the
other is a little lighter.

If slow old men use walking sticks,
what do fast old men use?

Hurry canes.

Which jeweler was the loudest?

The one who made
my earring.

If apple made a car what
would be missing?

Windows.

What do you get if a dinosaur
kicks you in the backside?

Megasoreass.

I told my doctor "yoga is the best antidepressant available".

"Sounds like a bit of a stretch", he replied.

As I looked at my naked body in the mirror...

I realised that I was going to get kicked out of IKEA.

Did you hear about the T-rex who sells guns?

He's a small arms dealer.

I accidently drank a
bottle of disappearing ink.

Now I'm sitting in the
ER waiting to be seen.

What do you call a lazy kangaroo?

A pouch potato.

How do you cut an ocean in half?

You use a Sea-Saw.

What do you call a herd
of giggling cows?

Laughing stock.

I'm really not a fan
of Russian dolls.

They're so full of themselves.

My dad always told me I should
marry an Egyptian woman

He said they make
great mummies.

My flashlight died.

I'm delighted.

My yoga instructor was
drunk today.

Put me in a very
awkward position.

I had a dream where I weighed
less than a thousandth of a gram.

I was like Omg.

What happens to an illegally
parked frog?

It gets toad.

What country is filled with
body builders?

Liftuania.

What do you call an ugly
dinosaur?

An eyesaur.

Maybe I should clean mirrors for a living.

It's something I can really see myself doing.

I hurt my bottom after shaking it at the office party.

It was a twerk-place injury.

Did you hear about the chameleon who couldn't change color?

He had a reptile dysfunction.

I saw a microbiologist today.

He was much bigger than I expected.

I need help. Someone glued my deck of cards together.

I don't know how to deal with it.

My neighbors listen to great music.

Whether they like it or not.

What do you call birds that
stick together?

Velcrows.

How much memory does a
mountain goat have?

About 4 legs of RAM.

Dad, can you tell me what a
solar eclipse is?

No sun.

Today I made my first money
as a Programmer.

I sold my laptop.

I applied for a job to be a spy.

They wanted my resume
and undercover letter.

You can't plant flowers.

If you haven't botany.

Made in the USA
Monee, IL
02 December 2022

19403874R00057